ECUADOR Road Trip

An Insider's Guide to Planning an Amazing Adventure

Jessamyn Salinas

Copyright © 2017 Jessamyn Salinas All rights reserved. No part of this publication may be reproduced, distributed, or transmitted in any form or by any means, including photocopying, recording, or other electronic or mechanical methods, without the prior written permission of the publisher, except in the case of brief quotations embodied in reviews and certain other noncommercial uses permitted by copyright law.

Dedication

I would like to dedicate this book to my parents. Their sense of adventure is what turned my life from ordinary to extraordinary!
Thanks for pushing us to be adventurous and to try new things!

Contents

DEDICATION

CHAPTER ONE

My Ecuador Adventure 1

SECTION ONE

Everything Ecuador 6

CHAPTER TWO

Why Visit Ecuador? 7

CHAPTER THREE

Basic Ecuador Facts 14

SECTION TWO

Planning Your Trip 21

CHAPTER FOUR

Before Leaving Home 22

CHAPTER FIVE

Arriving in Ecuador 35

CHAPTER SIX

Pros and Cons: Renting a Car 44

CHAPTER SEVEN

Road Trip by Bus 50

SECTION THREE

Where to Go 64

CHAPTER EIGHT

Suggested Routes 65

CHAPTER NINE

Mountain Places 74

CHAPTER TEN

Coastal Places 93

CHAPTER ELEVEN

Jungle Places 99

CHAPTER TWELVE

Food and Drink Checklist 103

SECTION FOUR

On the Road 107

CHAPTER THIRTEEN
What to Keep With You 108

CHAPTER FOURTEEN
Hotel Tips 113

CHAPTER FIFTEEN
Parking the Car 118

CHAPTER SIXTEEN
Precautions 120

CHAPTER SEVENTEEN
Some *Friendly* Tips 127

CHAPTER EIGHTEEN
Have a Great Time! 131

Chapter One
My Ecuador Adventure

In February of 1997, I moved to Ecuador with my family. I was 15 and the experience changed my life.

Our First Road Trips

At the beginning, we explored the country by bus. We saw many places, including small towns that most tourists will never see. Plus, the experience in itself is purely Ecuadorian. You get to see a part of the culture up close as you get from Point A to Point B.

I still remember our first ride on the bus from Guayaquil to San Miguel de Bolivar. It was Carnival, and I was sitting near the front, which meant I had to duck every time the door opened, otherwise I would get pelted with water balloons or doused with buckets of water laced with ink.

The buses back then had so much personality. The front dash would be covered in stickers, flashing

Insider's Guide

lights and religious statues. Thirty or so simple seats would accommodate twice that amount of people, with bodies being squashed into the aisles, kids sitting on laps and even the small open area behind the driver filled to beyond capacity.

Buses nowadays might not have the same amount of creative energy, but riding the bus is ALWAYS an experience.

People (and animal!) watching on the bus is always fun, because you never know what you will experience....

- Vendors selling anything and everything and/or giving speeches.
- A sack full of live chickens being lugged on board.
- Llamas being hauled onto the roof and then watching the shadows of their long necks swaying back and forth projected onto the roadside.
- A mother with her baby standing in the aisle of the bus. The baby isn't wearing a diaper and is sitting on the back of your seat—

Ecuador Road Trip

perilously close to your head.

- And, of course, Latin beats blaring from the radio.

*All true stories experienced by my family and me. :)

"Better" Transport

After about two years in Ecuador, my dad bought a '77 Land Rover. It was basically a tin can with an engine and it was great fun! The air vents along the floor let the puddles splash you as you went through them, and no power steering meant you got a

My family in front of the loaded-up Land Rover in 1998

Insider's Guide

workout while you were driving.

We spent many hours in that beast, enjoying the scenery, reciting Shakespeare and even spending the night on the roof in the middle of the jungle once!

During those first years, the roads were.... terrible. The few that were paved were dotted with potholes and the rest were glorified paths through the jungle or curving around the edge of steep river gorges.

We Still Love Road Trips

Today things are much improved and even those jungle paths are now wide paved highways.

About five years ago, my grandma came to visit us. We rented a car and started driving from Quito down the mountains into the jungle to my home in Tena. After a few days at my house we took a long road trip and drove about 700 miles (1,125 km) total around the country.

It is the best way to see the country!

My grandma kept her camera in hand at all times

and took over 1,000 photos. There were so many beautiful spots--how could anyone resist taking photo after photo?!

Ever since that first road trip we have taken one almost every year when my family comes to visit. In this way, we have seen much of the country. However, there's....

Still So Much More to See!

Even after living 13 of the last 20 years in Ecuador, I have realized that I may never see all that this beautiful place has to offer.

What I have seen, I've seen from the windows of buses and rental cars. I am still amazed at the natural artistry that surrounds me.

This book has been put together to help you plan and enjoy an Ecuador road trip. Whether you plan to go by bus, rent a car or hire a driver, the tips that follow will help make your trip a success.

I hope you enjoy your travels in Ecuador and that you love this beautiful spot on the planet as much as I do!

Insider's Guide

Section One

Everything Ecuador

In this section, learn a bit about this little South American country and why you NEED to come and see it!

"ALL IN ONE PLACE"

— ECUADOR'S MINISTRY OF TOURISM

Chapter Two

Why Visit Ecuador?

Ecuador is a tiny country in South America, often overlooked because of its larger, more popular neighbors like Peru, Colombia, Brazil and Argentina. It's definitely worth exploring though! Why?

There's so much packed into this little country. Part of the current slogan for the Ministry of Tourism in Ecuador is "All in One Place."

In a short period of time, you can go from the coast to the mountains to the jungle. Each region has a different climate and beautiful scenery, meaning that there is so much you can explore!

Even if you only have a long weekend, you can see several distinct places. Of course, a few weeks of vacation is even better. You will be amazed over and over again by the changing beauty all around you.

Traveling to Ecuador

You can travel from anywhere in North America to Ecuador in just one short day, and if you live in a city

Insider's Guide

with a direct flight (such as Miami) you can be there in as little as four hours. Traveling from Europe or other parts of the world will mean a longer trip, but I promise it will be worth it!

When Should You Plan Your Trip?

Ecuador's weather can be described as either "eternal spring" or "eternal summer" depending on the region. This means you can come to Ecuador any time of year. Take advantage of summer vacation or escape the brutal winters to visit Ecuador!

You will notice right away how green the countryside is. This is a direct result of the regular rains that Ecuador enjoys throughout the year. While you can definitely expect rain at some point during your trip, it will not be a complete washout.

During the first months of 2017, Ecuador has seen record rainfall all over the country due to a phenomenon known as the Niña Modoki. This is the second time in about 20 years that this has happened, but don't worry--you will still enjoy sunshine almost daily!

Ecuador Road Trip

La Casa del Arbol - Baños

Something for Everyone

Ecuador has such a variety of climates, activities and sights to see that anyone will enjoy vacationing here.

Families with small children or teenagers will find activities for their kids that will be entertaining and educational as they explore this new culture.

If you are traveling on a **budget**, there are tons of inexpensive food, lodging, transportation and tour options. Don't worry though--inexpensive doesn't mean that they aren't just as much fun or just as appealing!

Insider's Guide

If you want to enjoy the "high life", **luxury options** are available throughout the country.

Adventure Travel

Many people come to Ecuador for an adrenaline rush. There are plenty of options for adventure, including:

- Surfing
- Whitewater Rafting
- River and Sea Kayaking
- Paragliding
- Swing Jumping
- Cable cars
- Canyoning
- Jungle tours and more!

Culture, Culture, Culture

It's hard to define Ecuador's culture in just a few words. Each region has its own culture…actually there are multiple different cultures within each region. Exploring these differences is an enlightening experience that is full of fun along the way.

Appreciate colonial architecture, ancient ruins, markets, museums and art galleries, plus enjoy getting to know the genuinely friendly and helpful people that live here!

Nature

The beauty of current and previous peoples is only exceeded by the natural grandeur of Ecuador. I am still amazed at the magnificent surroundings of where I live.

Mt Chimborazo

Insider's Guide

Volcanoes, waterfalls, rivers, patchwork patterns on the hillside, paramo, mangroves, beaches, crater lakes, rainforest, even reefs. "All in One Place."

Within these natural features are a multitude of birds, animals and insects. People from all over the world come to birdwatch and see some of the thousands of species endemic to Ecuador. Humpback whales come to the coast of Ecuador once a year (from June to September) and put on spectacular displays. Cute, furry vicuñas, cousins of the llama, graze around the extinct Chimborazo volcano.

How to See Ecuador

You can enjoy all that Ecuador has to offer, no matter what your budget. In this book, we are going to talk about exploring the country on the bus or in a rental car.

The bus system in Ecuador is extensive and inexpensive, however the most unrestricted way to travel the country is by renting a car if you are able to. This way you can go where you want to on your own schedule.

Why Wait?

With so much to see and do in Ecuador, why are you waiting? Let's get started planning your trip! First, though, let's go over the basics and get to know the country a bit better.

Chapter Three

Basic Ecuador Facts

I've already mentioned the geographical diversity that exists in Ecuador. There are four main geographical regions, and while each is unique, the union of regions makes for many different sub-climates.

This variety has led to Ecuador being named one of the 17 most megadiverse countries in the world. Other countries on the list includes places like Australia, China, India, South Africa and the United States as well as many of Ecuador's South American neighbors.

According to Conservation International, Ecuador has the highest diversity per kilometer of any nation on Earth, meaning that there's lots to explore!

I'll go over each main region briefly and then mention some basic facts about Ecuador.

The Pacific Coast

The western side of Ecuador borders the Pacific

Ocean. The sandy beaches are interwoven with towering cliffs and both tropical and mangrove forests. Dry tropical forests are dotted with giant ceibo trees, while the flat inland areas are full of banana plantations and other tropical crops.

Along the way there are tiny fishing villages and a few bigger cities with a population of people who are known for being outgoing and friendly, as well as for their amazing culinary talents!

The climate on the coast is hot and humid. Part of the year is more overcast and cool (typically from May until December), while the rest of the year is sunny with frequent rains. Total rainfall is higher in the northern coast and steadily decreases as you head south.

The Andes Mountains

The Andes Mountains run straight down the middle of Ecuador in a line known as the "Avenue of the Volcanoes". Within these mountains about 50 volcanoes (in various stages of activity from extinct to dormant to active) can be found, including seven with a peak

Insider's Guide

Guaranda Central Park

elevation of more than 17,000 feet. The Pan-American Highway, which runs from Alaska to the tip of Chile, follows the Avenue of the Volcanoes as well, making for one beautiful road trip!

The majority of Ecuador's population lives in the mountains. Cities and towns of all sizes are found in the valleys and up the sides of the mountains.

The fertile soil produces a large array of crops including dozens of varieties of potatoes. The fields create a patchwork pattern up the mountains.

The mountains have many indigenous tribes. Those familiar with these people can easily determine where someone is from by the color of their poncho, the style of their hats or of the women's skirts.

The people of the mountains tend to be more reserved than they are in other parts of Ecuador, but while they may be a bit quiet, they are still very friendly.

The climate is spring-like year-round. The strong sun can burn your skin even though the air feels just warm, and the winds can be rather strong. Evenings tend to be cool. It does rain regularly with more frequent rains from December to March. At higher elevations snow even falls, but it usually melts with the sun, except on the highest of mountains.

The Amazon Jungle

Ecuador's third main region extends to the east of the Andes. Although it covers the largest area of the three regions it is the least densely populated.

This zone is lush and green, snaked with rivers and full of wildlife and natural beauty.

The cities are a mix of natives to the area and Ecuadorians from other parts of the country. Many

Insider's Guide

originally came to the area to work in oil companies, gold mines or other business opportunities.

Villages throughout the area are mostly populated with native tribes. The majority of these people work cultivating coffee, cacao and yuca in their fields, which they then bring into the bigger towns and cities to sell.

The jungle climate is hot and humid. The further away you get from the mountains the hotter it gets. Rain is to be expected almost daily...it is the rainforest after all.

The Galapagos

This final region of the country won't be reached on your "road" trip, but the Galapagos are part of Ecuador and an additional reason to come and visit. A quick flight from either Guayaquil or Quito brings you to these "Enchanted Islands."

The Galapagos continues with Ecuador's diversity theme. The Islands are famous for the variety of animals, some of which are found nowhere else on the planet, that call them home.

Ecuador Road Trip

The first half of the year is sunny and warm, where the second half is cooler and windier. Due to the Humboldt current, marine animals and birds are usually more active from June to November.

There are all-inclusive cruise options to tour the islands or you can do it on your own, budget style. There are numerous travel agencies in Quito and Guayaquil that offer last-minute deals. Please note that "Island-Hopper" tours aren't cruises, but land based tours which visit the three main islands via daily ferries.

Whether you go all-inclusive or do it on your own, you will be able to see the many species of endemic animals up close and enjoy an amazing, bucket list adventure.

Quick Facts

Population: 16.6 million

Capital City: Quito

Largest City: Guayaquil

Official Language: Spanish

Insider's Guide

Other Languages Spoken: 24 other languages including 9 dialects of Quichua

Area: 109,483 mi² (283,560 km²) --about the size of the state of Nevada in the USA

Number of Provinces: 24

Currency: US Dollar

Religion: Roman Catholic

Top Exports: Petroleum, bananas, cut flowers (roses and orchids), shrimp

Neighboring countries: Peru and Colombia

Section Two

Planning Your Trip

A successful vacation to Ecuador needs planning. Where should you start? What should you pack? Which airport should you fly into? All these questions and more will be answered here.

"OH, THE PLACES YOU'LL GO."

— DR. SEUSS

Chapter Four

Before Leaving Home

Now that you're convinced and you are ready to visit Ecuador...where do you begin?

Well, the first thing to check is your passport. **Ecuador requires six months validity on your passport.** There is no leniency on this--they will send you right back to your home country if you do not have at least six months left.

Will you need to apply for a visa prior to coming to Ecuador?

When entering Ecuador most people will be eligible for a 90-day tourist stamp (T-3). Exceptions include citizens of the following countries: Afghanistan, Bangladesh, Cuba, Eritrea, Ethiopia, Kenya, Nepal, Nigeria, Pakistan, Somalia, and Senegal. This has been known to change very quickly, so please check the requirements for your particular country before you begin your trip.

If you need a visa, contact the Ecuadorian Consulate

or Embassy nearest you for information on how to proceed.

What if you want to stay longer than 90 days? A 90-day extension is available which will allow you to extend your stay up to 180 days. You must apply for this extension and pay the applicable fee.

You can stay up to one year in Ecuador as a tourist with the T-3 stamp, the 90-day extension and an additional Special Tourist Visa which is valid for six months. You must be able to prove that you have the funds to be able to support yourself during your stay as you cannot work under any of the tourist options mentioned here.

The T-3 and 90-day extensions may only be used once every 365 days, and the Special Six-month Tourist Visa is only available once every five years.

Please note: It is now a governmental requirement that tourists on the 90-day extension or the Special Tourist Visa provide proof of health insurance that can be used in Ecuador. Keep in mind that although you must have health insurance, it won't be accepted as payment at most hospitals, doctors, etc. You will be expected to pay for any services at the

Insider's Guide

time they are rendered and turn the charges into your insurance company for reimbursement.

Vaccinations

Do you need to be vaccinated for certain illnesses before traveling to Ecuador? No vaccinations are required, but in addition to routine vaccines, the following should be considered:

- Hepatitis A - spread by contaminated food and drink.
- Typhoid - also spread in food and water.
- A current Tetanus shot.

You should also consider (depending on where you plan to travel in the country):

- Yellow Fever - spread by mosquitoes. There is a slight risk of yellow fever in areas deep in the jungle of Ecuador. Also, some nearby countries require proof of vaccination if you have been in Ecuador, even if you didn't travel to areas where the disease is endemic.
- Malaria prevention.

Ecuador Road Trip

At times, there are outbreaks of dengue fever in the tropical areas of Ecuador. While there is no vaccine for dengue, mosquito repellant and other precautions can help to prevent contraction.

Check with your doctor before you plan to visit and ask what vaccinations you should have, based on your current health.

Packing List

Keep in mind that the many climates within Ecuador mean the weather is constantly changing. Expect to experience both rain and sun. Temps range from the 50s to the 90s (F).

Here's what I would recommend bringing:

- Layers: long and short-sleeved tees, lightweight pants and shorts
- A warm jacket--it doesn't have to be a parka, but you'll want something for chilly evenings. If it's waterproof, even better!
- Any medications that you take on a regular basis. Medications here in Ecuador are usually dispensed over-the-counter, and

Insider's Guide

while they are generally much less expensive than in the US, they are not always available. Never leave your medication at home assuming that you'll be able to get it here-- that's not always the case. In addition, the laws regulating medications are evolving and may be different by the time you visit.

- Really good walking shoes. Maybe even an extra pair that's waterproof for wet days.
- Bathing suit for the ocean, rivers, and thermal pools.
- Hat, sunglasses and sunscreen. The equatorial sun is strong! Don't ruin your trip with a sunburn.
- Bug repellent. The mountains of Ecuador don't have many mosquitoes or other biting bugs, but the jungle and coast do.
- An umbrella or other rain gear. You can buy umbrellas in Ecuador but they tend to be very low quality and break easily. If you don't use an umbrella on a regular basis at home, feel free to gift it to someone before you leave to go home. :)

Ecuador Road Trip

- Ear plugs. Essential if you are a light sleeper. All night parties, roosters, barking dogs or car alarms may disturb your sleep.

- A jar of peanut butter or marmite. If your daily routine involves one of these foods (or if you want an option for an easy snack), you might want to bring a jar or two with you. Peanut butter can be found in Ecuador, but it's expensive. I don't think I've ever seen marmite in Ecuador, except in care packages sent to British and Australian friends. Note: Pack in your checked luggage. These items are sometimes considered liquids.

- A good book or two. If you really like to read, bring a book you don't mind leaving behind and exchange it at one of the many book exchanges found in tourist towns.

- A good Latin American Spanish phrasebook-- depending on your level of Spanish proficiency, of course.

- A flashlight and a pocket knife can also be of help at times.

- Don't forget your camera!

Insider's Guide

"Personally, I found traveling by backpack to be of huge help. Most cities are not roller suitcase friendly. The backpacks (65 liter for each of us) made transportation very easy."
- Jen Mitchell

Parents Traveling with Small Children

If you are traveling with kids that still use car seats, you will find that they aren't commonly used in Ecuador so you may want to bring yours from home. It is not advisable to plan on buying a car seat here, as they are extremely expensive (sometimes as much as 4 or 5 times the cost of the US) and can only be found in the larger cities.

If you bring a stroller, keep in mind that some areas of Ecuador have very uneven sidewalks. For the most part, a stroller can be handy to have if your kids tire of walking quickly. A hiking backpack is a good alternative if your little ones are still small enough to fit in one.

Ecuador Road Trip

My List

I have two items in addition to the ones above that I like to have when traveling in Ecuador. During your travels, you might experience some stomach upset. I personally use two natural products.

1. Grapefruit seed extract. Sold in liquid or tablet form. You can take this daily to prevent parasites or take a higher dosage if you suspect you have parasites. It can also be used to clean raw fruit and vegetables. KILOL, sold in Ecuador, is a diluted form of grapefruit seed extract.

2. Charcoal tablets. Great for an upset stomach. I take two after a meal that makes me feel nauseous and within a few hours feel much better.

Of course, if you are violently ill, see a doctor! These are just tips for minor stomach issues.

Money

When traveling Ecuador, you will have two payment options.

Insider's Guide

1. Paying in cash (most common). You will find that most places do not have change for big bills, so don't carry any bills larger than $20. If you have anything larger than that you will probably have to get them changed at a bank.
2. Paying with credit cards. Large stores, hotels, tour agencies and some restaurants will accept credit/debit cards. Make sure to let your credit card company know that you will be traveling internationally so that they don't think your card was stolen and freeze it. *Note: American Express and Discover cards are not widely accepted in Ecuador--you are better off with a Visa or Mastercard.

Travelers checks are a hassle in Ecuador and there are very few banks that will exchange them for you. I don't recommend using them.

ATMs are available throughout the country and work smoothly with most foreign credit and debit cards. Some banks (like the Banco de Pichincha) don't even charge withdrawal fees, but check with your bank for their international fees.

Ecuador Road Trip

How much money should you budget for your trip? You can travel Ecuador on the cheap or very lavishly. The following budget numbers are median prices just to give you an idea. You can find cheaper options as well as much more expensive ones.

- Hotels: $20 per person per night
- Food: $20 per person per day
- Tours: $50 per person
- Transportation: $10 per person per destination (This price is just to give you a ballpark idea of what you will spend on getting to your destination on the bus and then using taxis to get around. See car rental budgets in Chapter Six.)

Before you leave Ecuador, sift through the change you've accumulated. Ecuadorian versions of US coins will be mixed in. Try to use them up, since they won't be accepted in the States (not even in vending machines).

Bringing a Cell Phone

It's a good idea to have a phone while traveling in

Insider's Guide

Ecuador. You can make last minute hotel reservations, call for help or keep in touch with family and friends back home.

You have three options for having a cell phone in Ecuador:

1. Get an international plan through your current cell carrier. My dad was able to do this on his last trip to Mexico. It was great for his customers, but my mom would have probably preferred he just turned the phone off.

2. Get a SIM card for your cell phone. You can easily buy a mini, micro or nano SIM card at the major cell phone carriers in Ecuador. Please note that your phone must work on the 850 frequency and should be unlocked. There are many technicians in Ecuador that can unlock your phone, but there is no guarantee that every cell phone can be unlocked.

3. Buy a new phone for your trip. You can either buy a phone before traveling or when you arrive in Ecuador. Why would you want to

buy a new phone? Sadly, cell phones (especially iPhones) tend to be a target for thieves. Instead of bringing a really nice phone, you may want to get a cheap one just for your trip. If you buy a phone beforehand make sure it is GMS 850 or 3G. Please note that cell phones in Ecuador are NOT cheap. You will likely pay 200% or more compared to prices in other places, especially for smartphones. If you have bought a phone just for this trip you should be able to sell it easily before you leave Ecuador.

The main cell phone providers in Ecuador are Claro, Movistar and CNT. Each area of Ecuador has their preferred provider, and although Claro has the best coverage, any of the providers will work fine while you are in-country.

You can use a pay-as-you-go plan (*prepago*) and add call time and data packages as you need them.

Of course, if you think you can get by without having a phone by your side at all times, you could opt to just use Wi-Fi connections with apps like WhatsApp (very popular in Ecuador) and Skype.

Insider's Guide

There are also "*cabinas*" (phone booths) available at many places in Ecuador. There aren't as many as there used to be, but they are still around.

Did you forget your charger?

Hotels in Ecuador often have a stash of chargers that have been left behind. Just ask--chances are they have one that might work for your device. If they don't have the charger you need, local cellular and computer shops will often have universal chargers for sale.

Ecuador Road Trip

Chapter Five

Arriving in Ecuador

Traveling somewhere is exciting, but at the same time it can be unnerving. "What will happen?" "Will I run into trouble?" "Where do I go next?"

Let's run through what will happen when you arrive in Ecuador, step-by-step.

Airports

You will probably be flying into either Quito (UIO) or Guayaquil (GYE). Each airport has advantages depending on where you plan to travel.

Flying into Quito: Quito is central to most places in Ecuador. You can easily travel north and south through the mountains, east to the jungle or west to the coast.

Flying into Guayaquil: Guayaquil is more convenient if you are traveling exclusively to the south of Ecuador or along the coast.

Insider's Guide

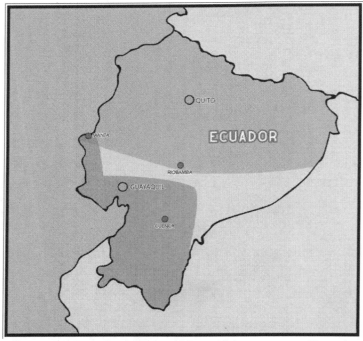

Choose your airport depending on which part of the country you will spend more time in or fly into one and out of the other.

You can also fly to other major cities in Ecuador from either international airport. Both Quito and Guayaquil are "final destination" airports, meaning you won't be making a connection there but rather changing airlines to fly inside the country.

Ecuador Road Trip

If you are flying to one of the smaller airports, plan to spend the night either at your arrival airport or in a hotel, since the smaller flights do not operate overnight. Ecuador isn't all that large so this probably won't be necessary unless you plan to spend the majority (or all) of your time in the far south part of Ecuador (i.e. Cuenca and Loja areas) or if you are visiting the Galapagos.

Immigration

On arrival at either airport, you will be directed to Immigration. Here your passport validity and visa will be reviewed. If you qualify to enter on the 90-day tourist stamp, it will be added to your passport at this time.

This process is usually quick and painless. Sometimes the line can be quite long, especially if several flights arrive at the same time, but it still tends to move quickly.

Customs

Once you've cleared Immigration, you will move on to pick up your checked luggage and then go through customs.

Insider's Guide

As is common on most international flights, you will have received (and hopefully filled out) the customs papers before arriving in Ecuador.

All luggage is screened by X-ray machines. Physical checks used to be more frequent, but are now only carried out if something suspicious is identified in your luggage or if you have something to declare.

What you need to know: If you have excess amounts of anything considered "personal items," you can be taxed; however, Customs agents are usually looking for electronics.

You are only allowed **one new** and **one used** of the following items per adult traveler:

- cell phones
- laptop computers
- tablets
- cameras

If you are found with more, you can be taxed. Current import tax rates are around 35%, but some travelers have reported being charged up to 100% of the value of their items, especially high-end electronics.

Other restrictions include (per adult traveler):

- 3 liters of alcohol
- 2 musical instruments
- 6 memory cards
- 10 video games
- 300 mL of perfume

Leaving the Airport

Quito's airport is about 20 km outside the city, whereas in Guayaquil the airport is close to hotels and the city center.

It's a good idea to have hotel reservations before you leave for Ecuador, at least for the first night or two of your stay. There are many good options in both cities at every price point.

With your confirmed reservation in hand, you have a few ways of getting to your destination:

1. **Rent a car.** If you plan to rent a car for your road trip, you could do this ahead of time and

Insider's Guide

pick up the rental as you leave the airport. However, many international flights arrive late into Ecuador (often after 11 p.m.) and some rental car agencies close by 10 p.m. or even earlier. Make sure the agency you choose knows when you will arrive and agrees to be there. Also consider that you may want to explore the city for a day or two, and probably won't need the car until you actually begin to travel around the country.

2. **Take a taxi.** There are registered taxi companies at both airports. Have the name and address of your hotel on hand. Ask for a quote before getting into the taxi. Airport agents can point you to the accepted taxi price list available inside the airport. Make sure that you are using a registered taxi (the registration will be visible on the side of the taxi). So-called "gypsy taxis" are unregulated and can be dangerous.

3. **In Quito, take the bus.** There is a bus service that takes you into downtown Quito. This service, called *AeroServicios*, can be handy especially if you want to save some cash, as a taxi can set you back $25 or more. The bus is comfortable, has plenty of room for baggage,

and costs just $8 one-way. This option is available from 4:30 a.m. until 9 p.m. during the week and from 5 a.m. until 11:30 p.m. on the weekends. The bus brings you to the site of the old Quito airport, which is closer to hotels and restaurants. You will probably still need to catch a taxi from there to your final destination.

4. **Arrange for pick-up with your hotel.** Most hotels will be glad to arrange for a taxi or van to pick you up. The cost is generally the same as a taxi. If you have made arrangements with the hotel, look for your name on the signs held up by drivers as you leave Customs.

The Key to Staying Safe

As I mentioned at the beginning of this chapter, arriving in a new place can be unnerving and Ecuador, like everywhere in the world, has its share of crime.

An important factor to not becoming easy prey for thieves is to walk and talk like you know what you're doing. This book is specifically designed to help you know what to expect and to plan out each step of your trip so that you can be mentally prepared.

Insider's Guide

The number one thing I always tell people is to be aware of your surroundings and know where you are heading. Try not to wander aimlessly, don't accept anything that someone tries to hand you on the street, don't flash expensive jewelry or electronics, and don't drink alcohol alone or accept drinks from strangers.

It is advisable to register with your embassy (or the embassy of the country handling diplomatic relations for your country) when you arrive. This is very simple to do and can be done online.

Keep your options open

Now that you've made it to Ecuador and to your hotel, rest up. The fun is about to begin!

Some people suffer adverse reactions to the altitude in Quito (9,000 ft/3,000 m above sea level). The altitude can give you a headache or cause you to feel nauseous and a bit "off". You may need to lay low for a day or two while your body adjusts. Many suggest drinking cinnamon tea sweetened with *panela* (unrefined cane sugar) for altitude sickness.

Ecuador Road Trip

"It's important to make sure you are drinking enough water as well. The air in Quito is very dry because of the high altitude and it doesn't take long to get dehydrated. A good rule of thumb is that you should need to use the restroom about once every two hours. If you're not, up your water intake. Bottled water is very inexpensive and is available everywhere."

- Cynthia Maloy

Next, let's look at the advantages and disadvantages of two road trip travel options: renting a car or taking the bus.

Chapter Six

Pros and Cons: Renting a Car

This is my preferred mode of transportation when traveling in Ecuador, however it's not right for everyone.

Basic Requirements

To rent a car in Ecuador you must:

- Be 18 years old or older
- Have a valid driver's license from your home country
- Have an internationally recognized credit card

Do you need an International Driver's License? No. Ecuador will accept an international driver's license as valid, however they prefer that tourists drive on their driver's licenses from their home country. If you are stopped by the police they will check that your license is valid.

Do you have to pay with a credit card? No, but you

Ecuador Road Trip

do need to have a credit card to confirm your reservation and to provide a deposit. When renting the car, you will be asked to sign a voucher for the deposit amount, but the voucher will be returned to you when you return the car.

Most cars in Ecuador have a manual transmission, so keep that in mind if you aren't comfortable driving a stick shift. On the most recent trip my dad made to Ecuador, he did rent an automatic SUV, but it's the first time in six years that he ended up with an automatic.

Most rental companies do not allow their cars to be

Exploring Muyuna just outside of Tena - 2015

Insider's Guide

driven over the border into Peru or Colombia.

In Ecuador, we drive on the right side of the road. Most street signs are similar in shape and color to their counterparts in other parts of the world, just with Spanish words.

Cons of Renting a Car

The most popular reason you will hear for NOT renting a car is: "Drivers in Ecuador are crazy!" And it's true, especially in the big cities.

When driving **you must be alert and drive defensively**. I once read that, "Ecuador's people are laid back and peaceful.... until they get behind the wheel of a car."

Big city driving can be scary anywhere, but when people do the unexpected so often that you come to expect it, it can be really stressful.

One thing to note is that although drivers in Ecuador may scare you, it isn't like driving in places like New York City or Los Angeles where people are just mean and you are worried some impatient driver might pull out a gun. The stress involved when driving in

Ecuador Road Trip

Ecuador has more to do with unexpected maneuvers or strange behavior (like not turning their lights on unless it's completely dark or passing in a no passing zone).

*Keep in mind that although pedestrians "legally" have the right of way, most drivers will not yield for you as you cross the street. Use crosswalks and traffic lights to cross safely--it's not worth getting run over to save a couple of minutes' time.

I've been with a number of friends that have driven for years and years in Ecuador and other parts of the world that still get nervous when they drive into Quito or Guayaquil.

Counting the Cost

Another downside is the cost. Renting a car can be expensive, especially for weeks at a time. For a two-week trip, you can expect to pay between $700 and $1,000, depending on the size of vehicle and the amount of insurance coverage you want.

If you end up being involved in an accident in Ecuador, there is a law stating that if you are unable to reach an agreement with the other party, both parties can be put in jail. This shouldn't be a big deal since with the help of the police you should be able to work something out, but it's good to keep in mind.

Private Driver

If you would prefer to have your own vehicle, but want to avoid the scary driving and the accountability that comes with an accident, there are also services where you can rent a car with a driver. The cost for that is higher than renting a car, as you are usually expected to pay for the driver and his meals and lodging. However, if you are nervous about driving yourself, the additional cost may be worth it for you.

An added bonus of using a driver is that they will be familiar with the area you are traveling to and will be able to point out things of interest as you are traveling.

The Pros

With all those "cons" you might be thinking, "Is it worth it?" I say, if you have the money and a level head when driving, go for it!

Ecuador Road Trip

Why? The ease and comfort of traveling when and where you want can be invaluable. You can make your own schedule and stop whenever you need to whether to take a photo or go to the bathroom.

Chapter Seven
Road Trip by Bus

A long bus ride is a part of life in Ecuador. I recently met an Ecuadorian woman in her late 50s who said she had never been on the bus before. I had to pick my jaw up off the floor. **Everyone** rides the bus here at some point or another, even the woman mentioned above.

A Bit About the Bus System

When riding the bus, you will most likely go to one of the many bus terminals. Most cities have one main terminal. One exception is Quito which has two terminals with buses going in opposite directions. If you are traveling north (Otavalo, Cotacachi, etc.), catch the bus at the Carcelén Terminal. For the rest of the country, most buses leave from the Quitumbe Terminal in South Quito. There is a bus that connects the two terminals.

When arriving at the bus terminal there will be people shouting out destinations who can point you to the next bus heading that way. These salesmen

Ecuador Road Trip

can be a bit pushy trying to get you on their bus, so if you already have a ticket for another bus or for some other reason don't want that bus, hold your ground.

Inside the terminal, you will find many small offices/windows for each bus co-op. The offices are usually organized so that buses going in similar directions are nearby each other. The bus schedules are clearly posted at each office. Buy a ticket for the bus you want last-minute or up to several days ahead of time.

Fares are the same for both foreigners and Ecuadorians. Seniors, the disabled and children pay half price on most buses.

Your bus ticket will have the departure time and date, the bus number and your seat number. Tickets are non-refundable. If for some reason, you can't travel and want to get a refund, go well before the departure time on your ticket and see if you can have your ticket sold to someone else. If you miss your bus, they won't refund your money.

When boarding the bus, find your seat which is clearly noted on the ticket. If there is someone in the

Insider's Guide

seat, just show them your ticket and they will move.

Once the bus leaves the terminal, the bus attendant will come through asking for tickets or for money from those who don't have tickets. The attendants are very helpful if you aren't sure where to get off the bus. Just let him know and he will call out your stop once you arrive.

As you get comfortable with the bus system you may choose to board the bus outside of the terminal, especially in cases where a bus travels a long distance through a big city. Example: When leaving Quito for Tena, the bus can take up to two hours to get from the Quitumbe Terminal to the road that actually heads to Tena. For this reason, we like to board the bus in one of the outer suburbs of Quito to save a bit of time. Just make sure you are waiting in the right place and know that without a ticket you may not get a seat.

The bus is a great way to travel in Ecuador for many reasons. For example...

Extensive Routes

There are buses to just about every corner of the

country. Only the most remote villages have no bus service and that's probably because there are either very few people living there or there is no road. This means that you can go almost anywhere in Ecuador by bus and the roads are reasonably good.

Inexpensive

Another upside to taking the bus is that it doesn't cost much. On average, you will pay about $1 per hour on the bus. You can go from one end of the country to the other for less than $30.

Comfortable

Buses today are nothing like the rickety things we used to ride 20 years ago. Nowadays, you will enjoy modern buses with comfortable seats, large windows, and sometimes (depending on where you're traveling) air conditioning.

A lot of buses will advertise Wi-Fi and bathrooms, but that's usually just hype. Some buses DO have a bathroom at the back of the bus, but the common response when you ask to use it is that it is broken or locked. Make sure to use the restroom before you get

Insider's Guide

Bus zipping through the mountains near Quito

on the bus...it might be hours before you have a good opportunity to use one again.

Punctual

In a country where everything can wait until later, the bus system is the exception to the rule. Buses always leave on time, and once they leave the city or town of origin, they make good time. Unless there is some inconvenience beyond their control, buses arrive within the stated number of hours.

Large cities or popular destinations will have

multiple bus companies that service that route. This means there will be a bus leaving every hour or sometimes even every half hour.

Culture Watch

The bus can also be a fun way to see some of the culture of Ecuador up close.

As you travel through different areas, vendors will get on the bus offering a variety of treats. Some are traditional foods of the area. An example would be as you travel between Ambato and Quito people board the bus selling "*allullas*". These wheat buns cooked in pork lard are unique to this area and you may not see them sold anywhere else in Ecuador.

People from all social levels and backgrounds get on the bus. You will see colorful native dress, modern teenage cockiness and beautiful, friendly faces everywhere and you never know what will come up those steps next. Animals, musicians, and travelers from all over the world love to ride the bus!

This mix of people can be interesting, but it can also be a downside of traveling on the bus...

Insider's Guide

Just One More Passenger

Buses can get quite crowded. I've been amazed at the number of people that sometimes squeeze into a bus. Even if you are sitting, the throngs in the aisles can crowd in and invade your personal space, bringing with them smells that you might not care for. It often reminds me of the Dial soap commercials of the 80s. "Aren't you glad you use Dial?"

There are laws in place that limit the maximum passenger capacity, usually according to the number of seats available, however this law isn't always followed, especially outside of the larger cities and during holidays.

Car Sick on the Bus

Another drawback to riding the bus is motion sickness. Before I moved to Ecuador, I would get sick when traveling into the mountains near my home in Colorado. The winding roads of my first home are found everywhere in Ecuador.

I actually think the improved road conditions have added to my car sickness. Riding on smooth, curvy

Ecuador Road Trip

roads in a tall "tin can" where you can't see out the front window is the perfect recipe for disaster!

If you do get car sick, try the following:

- When buying bus tickets ask for the first seat on the same side as the door if possible. Many of the new buses have a tinted window-wall between the driver and the passengers, but the door to the front opens often and sometimes you can see enough of the road in front of you to cope. If there is a curtain between the passengers and the driver you can explain to the driver that you get sick and ask him to open the curtain.

- Bring hard candy. Sucking on something sweet helps me.

- Ask to sit up front next to the driver. Most drivers don't want to have to deal with cleaning up vomit or stopping to allow you to get off the bus so if you ask, he might let you sit up next to him.

- Try to sleep.

- There are motion sickness pills available at

Insider's Guide

>any pharmacy. Just be careful, especially if you are traveling alone, as these pills can make you very drowsy and you could miss your stop or become a target for thieves.

- If you are going to be sick, yell "*funda*." This will send the bus driver's helper back to you with a plastic "barf bag". Some will have the bags hanging in the front of the bus.

Movie Time

This may be a positive point for some, but it's definitely a negative for me. Every time the TV comes on I cringe.

Ninety percent of the time the movie chosen by the driver is either violent, immoral, or demonic. Recently my husband had to get up and ask the driver to turn off the movie because it was pornographic.

Depending on the length of your trip, one or two movies will probably be shown. If possible, bring a few movies with you (you can buy cheap DVDs all over Ecuador for $1-1.50) and ask your driver to put them on. They will usually agree.

Ecuador Road Trip

If you do bring your own movies they should be in Spanish or at least have Spanish subtitles. DVDs bought in other countries don't usually work in DVD players sold in Ecuador. Taking into account that there are inevitably children traveling, comedies and family movies are usually a good choice.

Destiny

What?!?

Many Ecuadorians are Catholic and firmly believe in destiny. Due to this belief, they think there is nothing they can do to speed up or delay the appointed time of their death. This can lead to crazy driving. The thought process is that since there is no way to change your destiny, you can drive however you want to and it won't make any difference.

What to do if you have a scary driver

Sometimes buses will decide to race each other and this has led to many accidents. Others are just racing the clock. What can you do if you feel like your life is in danger?

- Call the police. 911 now works throughout

Insider's Guide

> Ecuador. You will be connected to the local police nearest to your current location.

- Call the number listed inside the bus. Most buses now have an emergency contact number on the partition between you and the driver.

- Tell the driver to "cut it out." ("*Basta!*") This will work with some drivers but not all. Threatening to call the police may help.

Some suggest taking down driver and bus information before beginning your journey. This way you have all the information you need beforehand in case you do need to call the police. Also, this alerts the driver that you are serious about your safety and will act if you feel threatened.

Another scary situation that happens, although not as often as it used to, is having your driver fall asleep. If you think your driver is falling asleep, go up and sit next to him. Try to have a conversation with him.

Thankfully, long trips now require that more than one driver be on the bus. This way they take turns and no one driver should be overly tired while behind the wheel.

Traveling at Night

One way to avoid overly tired drivers is to not travel at night. Some also suggest avoiding night buses due to increased possibilities of bus robberies. I haven't heard of any cases of robberies for a long time, but it is something that can happen.

There are some long-distance buses that travel overnight and even have sleeper chairs. These buses usually don't pick up additional travelers along the way, so you can sleep and you don't have to worry about criminals boarding the bus.

Traveling During Holidays

Thousands of Ecuadorians travel by bus during national holidays. If you are planning to travel during the holidays, it's a good idea to get a ticket ahead of time. This is the only way to guarantee a seat on the bus.

Here are some popular holidays in Ecuador when many people travel:

Insider's Guide

- New Year's Eve
- Carnaval (usually in February - the weekend before Ash Wednesday)
- Semana Santa (the week leading up to Easter)
- Day of the Dead/Independence of Cuenca (November 2nd and 3rd)
- Christmas (depending the day of the week Christmas falls on people usually have a few days off before and after)

Another time to avoid travel is the weekend of an election in Ecuador. Since all Ecuadorians are required to vote, many have to travel to the city where they are registered. Typically, elections are held in mid-February every five years.

City Buses and Trolleys

All cities and large towns in Ecuador have an urban bus system. These buses are a great way of getting across town. The main destinations will be posted in the front window of the bus. To be sure you get on the right one, ask at your hotel which bus to catch, where to wait for it and how much it costs. Some cities also provide maps of their bus and trolley

Ecuador Road Trip

routes.

Buses and trolleys tend to be very crowded and you may end up standing. Watch out for pickpockets and be extra careful when riding after dark!

All in all, riding the bus is part of the Ecuadorian experience. It's a great way to see the country no matter what your budget. Even if you choose to rent a car, you may want to try the bus at some point during your trip.

Insider's Guide

Section Three

Where to Go

Part of planning your trip includes deciding where you want go. You probably won't be able to see it all in one trip, but good planning can help fit in lots of unique places.

"I haven't been everywhere, but it's on my list."

— Susan Sontag

Ecuador Road Trip

Chapter Eight

Suggested Routes

It's great to have a plan before you start your road trip but don't set it in stone! Leave some wiggle room for exploring and for unexpected happenings.

What could happen to throw your trip off course? Well, it may (read "probably will") take you longer than you think to get where you're going, especially if you're driving yourself and you "accidentally" take a detour. You could run into a landslide or an accident. Your choice route may be blocked by road construction, a strike or a parade. Or maybe you just found a spot that you LOVE and want to stay longer than you planned!

Take your time. You're on vacation! Let it all soak in.

Also, remember that because of the Andes mountains it takes longer than you might imagine to get from one place to another. For example, the trip from Tena to Quito is about 120 miles (200 km), but it will take you about four hours in a car or five to six

Insider's Guide

in the bus due to the winding road that goes from just under 2,000 feet above sea level up to about 14,000 feet and then back down to 9,350 feet above sea level.

Keeping in mind that your destination may take longer to reach than you expected, it's a good idea to have two final destinations in mind per day, especially if you're driving yourself. If you are tired when you reach the first place on your list, stop. If you're feeling OK and there is still time, head on to place #2.

It would be impossible to cover EVERY interesting place in Ecuador. In most tourist towns, you will find an iTur tourism office. They have maps and suggestions for local activities and must-see spots.

The following pages contain popular routes you may enjoy. These are just some of the highlights of Ecuador. There are lots of towns, cities, mountains and beaches in between!

For more information on the places listed on the maps see the next three chapters.

So much to see! So little time!

Ecuador Road Trip

Northern Ecuador

Quito - Otavalo - Cotacachi - Ibarra - Tulcán

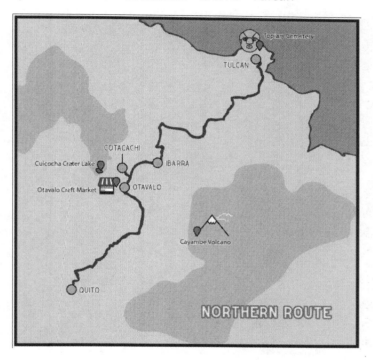

This route has amazing mountain scenery, the most popular market in Ecuador, traditional ice cream, leather goods, crater lakes and an ornate cemetery. Step over to Ipiales, Colombia if you're making a South American Tour.

Insider's Guide

North-Central Ecuador

Quito - Mitad del Mundo - Mindo

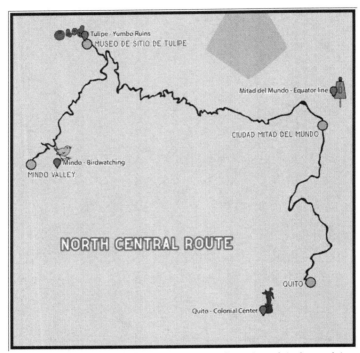

Visit the equator monument and enjoy birdwatching, waterfall hikes and quiet Ecuadorian living in the cloud forest.

Ecuador Road Trip

Central Ecuador

Ambato - Guaranda - Mt Chimborazo - Riobamba - Baños

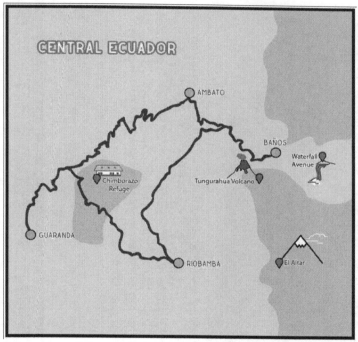

See some of the most impressive mountains of Ecuador, as well as waterfalls and outdoor activities such as kayaking, hiking, bicycling and mountain climbing.

Insider's Guide

South-Central Ecuador

Quito - Ambato - Riobamba - Alausí

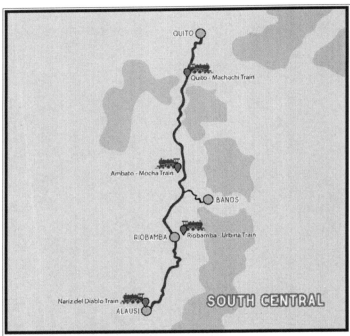

Ride the trains that used to connect Ecuador.

Ecuador Road Trip

Southern Ecuador

Ingapirca - Cuenca - Loja - Vilcabamba

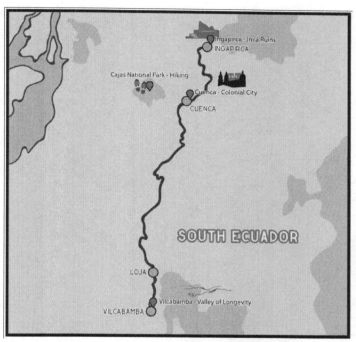

Visit Ecuador's best Incan ruins and beautiful colonial cities as well as Ecuador's own "Valley of Longevity."

Insider's Guide

Eastern Ecuador

Quito - Tena - Baños - Ambato - Cotopaxi Park

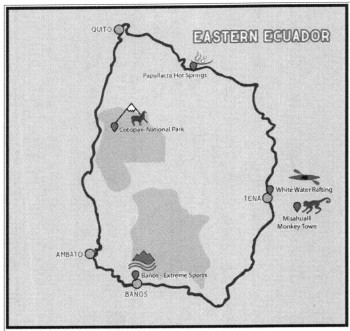

Within this circle enjoy thermal pools, white water rafting, jungle tours and lots of waterfalls. Great for nature lovers!

Ecuador Road Trip

Western Ecuador

Guayaquil - Salinas - Montañita - Puerto López - Manta - Bahía de Caráquez - Canoa

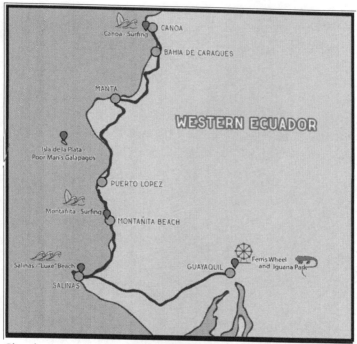

Check out the best beaches in Ecuador, as well as humpback whales and the "Poor Man's Galapagos."

Insider's Guide

Chapter Nine

Mountain Places

There are so many places to explore in the Andes of Ecuador. Here we will look at popular destinations in alphabetical order.

Alausí

Alausí is a tiny town between Riobamba and Cuenca. The town is a great place to see every day, small town life in Ecuador, with its narrow streets and

The Devil's Nose train going through Alausí

people in traditional dress meeting up to gossip in the central square. The main attraction here is the "Devil's Nose" (*Nariz del Diablo*) train ride which is an amazing feat of engineering.

Must See:
- The Devil's Nose

We really loved the Devil's Nose trip. At first, we almost skipped it, because it isn't the cheapest activity we've done in Ecuador.

We are all glad we went! It was fun, the views were amazing and there was an entertaining traditional dance demonstration! The ticket price included a small meal at the lower train station, and stopping in Alausí was a great way to break up the long car ride between Riobamba and Cuenca.

Ambato

Ambato is a large city; however, it is often overlooked as people pass through it (or around it on the bypass) on their way to bigger attractions in Quito and Baños.

Insider's Guide

Must See:

- In February, Ambato has their annual "Fruit and Flower Festival." This festival celebrates the fertile soil of the area and the resilience of the people of Ambato after a huge earthquake devastated the area in 1949. The parade for this event draws people from all over the country.

More Places to See:

- Homes of famous Ecuadorians Juan Leon Mera and Juan Montalvo.
- If you are traveling with small children a picnic at Ambato's "Parque de la Familia" (Family Park) can be a relaxing way to pass an afternoon while enjoying great views of the area.

Baños

Baños is one of Ecuador's most visited spots both by local and foreign tourists. This little town exists in the shadows of the active Tungurahua Volcano and has lots of fun outdoor activities.

Ecuador Road Trip

Must See Spots:

- "La Casa del Arbol" tree swing has amazing views and a great photo opportunity (see page 9) for just a dollar per person.

- "Waterfall Avenue" is the road between Baños and Puyo and has some amazing waterfalls. There are lots of options for exploring this road. Go by bike, go-kart, bus, *chiva*, or car. Don't miss the *"Manto de la Novia"* or the *"Pailón del Diablo"*.

- Baños Thermal Pools. Heated by the volcano, these pools are a great way to relax. The water is yellow due to the minerals it contains. We personally prefer the Salado pools.

Other Attractions:

- Baños is a great place for adventure travel and extreme sports. See a tour agency for rafting, swing jumping, canyoning and more!

- There are a variety of restaurants and lodging options that make Baños a great spot to stop for a few days.

Insider's Guide

Baños from the Bella Vista Overlook

 ***Don't skip Baños! On almost any road trip we take, we go to Baños and love it every. single. time. Whether you want to relax or have the adventure of a lifetime, Baños has it all!***
We love the fun vibe of the town. Places like Casa Hood Restaurant and Abby's Hideaway make for the perfect vacation.

Cotacachi

This small town is famous for its leather goods. It's a

Ecuador Road Trip

great place to buy gifts, as well as cowboy boots, hats, purses and other quality leather goods. While many shops do take credit cards, it is advisable to pay cash for your purchases. This gives you the added advantage of being able to "bargain" on the prices as well as protecting your credit card.

Must See:

- Cuicocha Crater Lake

"Cotacachi has a 5-star resort called La Mirage, with first class service and accommodations. The meals that they serve, from the music boxes that contain the appetizers to the sorbet that is served between courses, are second to none. If you go there, you have to try the lavender cake!"

- Joellen Nienaber

Cuenca

Cuenca has become popular due to the large number of expats who are now living there. It's a beautiful big city with parks, shops and colonial architecture.

Insider's Guide

Downtown Cuenca

Must See:
- Ingapirca, just a short journey north of Cuenca, is home to the best Incan ruins in Ecuador.

More Places to See:
- Take the city bus tour up to the Turi Overlook
- Visit the Central Bank Museum, complete with Incan ruins and a botanical garden in the backyard. It's free!
- Visit Cajas National Park. This beautiful reserve has lots of hiking trails to explore.

Ecuador Road Trip

- See the neighboring market towns of Gualaceo, Chordeleg and Sigsig.

 *I've been to Cuenca twice. I was really impressed by how a city this large could be so clean!*

We really liked the Cuenca Bus Tour which you will find at Parque Calderón right in the center of the city. It's a great way to see the sights without walking miles and miles. The Turi overlook also has impressive views of the city.

Ingapirca is also really cool! Amazing example of Incan engineering!

Guaranda

Guaranda is a quintessential mountain town hardly disturbed by tourists. The road to Guaranda from Ambato or Riobamba circles the extinct Chimborazo volcano. Watch for vicuñas, which are a cousin to llamas, along the way.

Must See:

Insider's Guide

- Visit the lowest Chimborazo climbing refuge. You can drive up and feel the cool, thin air of the mountain that reaches the farthest into the atmosphere when measured from the center of the Earth. The Refuge is at 16,000 feet, so don't plan on walking too fast--the air is very thin and you will be moving much slower than you're used to.

More to see:

- The small town of Salinas makes some of the best cheese in Ecuador. Tour their factory or visit their store in Guaranda for a variety of cheeses and chocolates.

During our first year and a half in Ecuador, we lived about 30 minutes from Guaranda, so this little town has a special place in my heart. I love that it is almost untouched by tourism, allowing you to observe pure Ecuadorian mountain culture.

We made this just a day trip on our last road trip. We left Baños in the morning and drove to Ambato and then on to Guaranda.

Ecuador Road Trip

Cute vicuñas are everywhere near Mt Chimborazo

After lunch in Guaranda and a short walk around town, we drove to the Chimborazo Refuge, circled all the way around Chimborazo to Riobamba and then back to Baños. It was a long day in the car, but the beautiful things we saw were worth every minute!

Ibarra

This northern Ecuadorian town is famous for its *"Helados de Paila"*, which are ice creams made in a special copper bowl. There is also a large lake called Laguna Yahuarcocha where you can enjoy outdoor activities. Nearby craft towns and hot springs are

Insider's Guide

also of interest.

Loja

Loja is a beautiful, thriving college town in southern Ecuador. Make sure to get a photo at the *"Puerta de la Ciudad"* (The City Gate).

Must See:

- If you are in Loja in January, check out the *Guayacán* trees that flower once a year. During this natural phenomenon, the entire forest turns yellow.

Mindo

Mindo is just a few hours north of Quito and to me is like a mini Baños. Mindo is popular with birdwatchers and has some great hiking trails that lead to waterfalls in the area.

- The butterfly farm, which is a lot of fun to visit with children.
- Try tubing or zip-lining.
- Visit the nearby Tulipe ruins.

Ecuador Road Trip

Steps to the Reina Waterfall in Mindo

Otavalo

Otavalo has the most famous market in all of Ecuador. The expert craftsmen of Otavalo have become famous worldwide. Otavalo is just about 15 minutes from Cotacachi and it's very easy to do both in the same day.

Must See:

- Otavalo's market. Saturday is the "official" market day, but you can see great crafts every day of the week.

Insider's Guide

- Visit the Mojanda lakes and the Peguche waterfall.

"When visiting the Peguche waterfall, be sure to stop in the shops in the village of Peguche. You can watch how weaving used to be done on old fashioned wooden looms, and even see how they created the different colors that were used."

- Joellen Nienaber

The Otavalo Craft Market

Ecuador Road Trip

"While you are in Otavalo, be sure to have lunch at the Pie Shop, located right on the square. They are known for their amazing chicken salad and incredible variety of pies. Service is a bit slow and seating is limited, so get there early!"

- Cynthia Maloy

Quito

Ecuador's capital city. You will likely be in Quito at some point and there are lots of things to see.

Must See Spots:

- Mitad del Mundo and/or the Intiñan Solar Museum. Both spots say they mark the equator; both are a tad bit off. These are still great spots for fun photos and their museum displays, as well as the restaurants that feature wonderful Ecuadorian cuisine. Try Yaravi, and get the llapingachos!

Insider's Guide

"When visiting the Indian museum next to Mitad del Mundo (Intiñan) bring your passport and have it stamped with a zero degrees latitude Ecuador stamp."
- Todd Gorishek

- Old Town Quito and "El Panecillo". A great way to see this area is on the Quito Bus Tour which goes to the tops spots in Quito's Historic District. There are also free walking tours available. The Panecillo is in the center of Quito and offers amazing 360° views of the city.

More Places to See:

- Check out the Teleferiqo cable car which takes you up the side of the Pichincha Volcano.

- Visit the Mariscal district (also known as *Gringolandia*) and Plaza Foch for good eats and nightlife. There is a great market in this neighborhood with a wide variety of souvenirs. Recommended restaurants include The Magic Bean (an icon!) and Uncle Ho's.

Ecuador Road Trip

- Quito has many large parks including Carolina Park which is a great place to relax or play sports, and El Ejido Park which has an arts and crafts market on the weekends. Local artists have their work for sale here and it is a great place to find amazing artwork for reasonable prices.

- The nearby Cotopaxi National Park gets you close to a beautiful, snow covered volcano.

View of Quito from the Basilica bell tower in Old Town

Insider's Guide

- Papallacta Thermal Pools. About a 90-minute drive outside of Quito, these are some of the most beautiful thermal pools in Ecuador. There are several places to choose from in town, but the most popular (and most expensive) are Termas Papallacta.
- Quilatoa Loop. This is a beautiful crater lake a few hours outside of Quito. Enjoy hiking and horseback riding around the lake.
- Another great day trip from Quito are the Tulipe ruins not far from Mindo.

Quito is another place with a great city bus tour. You can catch the bus at any of the stops along the route, get off where you want, explore the area and then get back on the bus to continue the tour. I loved getting to know this city this way!

Mitad del Mundo might feel like a bit of a tourist trap but it's still fun to visit. Next door at the Intiñan Solar Museum there are some fun activities that are great if you're traveling with kids--or even if you're not. On the weekends, there are cultural events held at Mitad del Mundo, including traditional dances and performances by local artists.

I also really like the market in the Mariscal. Whether you get to the Otavalo or not, this market has a huge array Ecuadorian handicrafts.

My dad doesn't like to drive in Quito if he can avoid it. This city is in a long narrow valley and this can cause quite a bit of traffic congestion. If you are just passing through to other parts of the country, it is easy to bypass the entire city center.

Riobamba

Another one of Ecuador's big cities, Riobamba is surrounded by impressive mountains. You used to be able to take the train from Riobamba to the Devil's Nose, but this trip is no longer available. There is another train option available in Riobamba which explores the culture and beauty of the area.

Tulcán

The last stop in Ecuador before crossing over into Colombia, Tulcán is famous for their cemetery full of interesting topiaries.

Insider's Guide

Vilcabamba

Just south of Loja, Vilcabamba is the famed "Valley of Longevity" and boasts many centenarians.

Ecuador Road Trip

Chapter Ten

Coastal Places

Here are some of the standout places on Ecuador's Pacific coast. Check out lots of other little towns and cities in between. If you enjoy crowds and action, the beach is the place to be during holidays--and if you like things a bit quieter, plan your beach vacation for the "off season".

Atacames

Atacames is one of Ecuador's top beach destinations. During Ecuadorian holidays, the place is packed! There's always a party going on.

"Find yourself a "batido de coco" (essentially a coconut "milkshake") and a spot on the sand and enjoy the beauty of the ocean."

- Cynthia Maloy

Insider's Guide

Bahía de Caráquez seen from the other side of the bay

Bahía de Caráquez

Known for being Ecuador's first "green city," Bahía is a popular mid-sized city jutting out into the bay between the Pacific Ocean and the mouth of the Chone River. The beach is small and nothing special.

Canoa

Canoa is the perfect mix of fun and quiet. The beach is popular with surfers and families alike.

Ecuador Road Trip

Canoa Beach

Must Try:

- Seafood recipes of Manabí. The province of Manabí is famous for their culinary creations. Try the *encocado*--you'll never be the same!

 *about it!* We love, love, love Canoa! We spent a relaxing few days there a few years back; eating great food and enjoying the ocean. I can't wait to go again! We were the first clients at the Canoa Beach Hotel and loved everything

Insider's Guide

> **A quick note about the earthquake**: On April 16, 2016, a 7.8 magnitude earthquake shook the northern coast of Ecuador affecting the aforementioned towns. Although there was extensive damage, most tourist areas have recovered and are ready (and anxious!) for business.

Guayaquil

Ecuador's biggest city has gone through a transformation over the last couple of decades, starting with its now famous boardwalk.

Must see:

- *"Malecón 2000"*. This stretch along the Guayas River has lots of shops, restaurants and its most recent addition--a giant ferris wheel.

- *"Las Peñas"* neighborhood. This colorful area at the end of the boardwalk climbs up to the *Cerro Santa Ana* above the city for some great views.

More to see:

Ecuador Road Trip

- Check out the *Parque Historico* (Historic Park) and the Botanical Gardens of Guayaquil.

- See iguanas up close at the *"Parque Seminario"*, also known as the Iguana Park.

I've been to Guayaquil many times in the past, but for the most part we were there just to catch an airplane. Since then Guayaquil has really reinvented itself and I'm looking forward to visiting again soon.

Montañita

This beach town is known for surfing, paragliding and lots of parties.

Olón

Montañita's quiet next-door neighbor is perfect if you are looking for less party and a nice beach. Friends of mine lived in Olón for a year. They raved about the beautiful beach!

Puerto López

A small town which may not seem to have much to

Insider's Guide

offer, however nearby attractions are worth the trip to this little fishing village.

Must see spots:

- Machalilla National Park with its *Frailes* beach is a big draw. During whale season (June through September), watch for humpbacks in the ocean.
- "*Isla de la Plata*", also known as the "Poor Man's Galapagos" is a great place for nature lovers and for seeing some of the same animals as found on the Galapagos.

Salinas

Another one of Ecuador's most popular beaches. Salinas can go from crowded at peak times to almost a ghost town at other times.

Places to see:

- Punta Carnero beach is popular with surfers.
- Take tours to see the whales from June until September.

Chapter Eleven

Jungle Places

As Ecuador's least populated area, the Amazon region has lots of nature to offer. See these main cities and areas that attract tourists.

Cuyabeno

See the jungle up close in the Cuyabeno Nature Reserve. Tours start from Lago Agrio (also known as Nueva Loja) which can be reached by car, bus or plane.

Macas

Rafters and kayakers come to Macas for the Upano River.

Puyo

A bigger city located between Macas and Tena. They have a water park and the "balsa wood factory" where you can purchase the famous balsa wood crafts that you see at the markets--the birds are

Insider's Guide

The Jungle just outside of Tena

especially colorful and fun.

Check out:

- The paths along the river are fun to explore.

Tena

Tena is a great place to see some jungle if you are short on time and/or money. Rafting and kayaking are popular due to the various rivers.

Ecuador Road Trip

Must see spots:

- Raft the Jondachi and/or the Jatunyacu Rivers.

- Visit Misahuallí and its resident monkeys. Here you can take short canoe rides to indigenous villages. The *Latas* Waterfall is beautiful!

- See the *"Laguna Azul"* ("Blue Lagoon"). It's not blue, but it is beautiful!

More to see and do:

- Visit the zoo in Archidona for a nice "jungle" walk and to see rescued animals from the area.
- Climb the spiral bridge in the center of Tena and explore the *Parque Amazonico* next door.
- There are several jungle lodges in the area.

I have lived in Tena for almost 13 years now. I love it here for many reasons. The weather is the perfect balance of heat and rain, with cool evenings.
There are lots of fun places to explore. I especially recommend the Laguna Azul

Insider's Guide

and river rafting. "River People Rafting" is run by friends of mine and is one of the most experienced rafting companies in Tena. They also have fun jungle tours.

Misahuallí is also entertaining. Bring an egg and an onion for the monkeys. :)

Chapter Twelve

Food and Drink Checklist

Here are some dining experiences you can enjoy while in Ecuador. See how many you can fit in.

Breakfast:

- ☐ *Majado de verde* - Mashed plantains served with eggs and sausage
- ☐ *Encebollado* - Fish and onion soup
- ☐ *Colada de avena/Quaker* - A thick drink made from oatmeal mixed with fruit

Lunch/Dinner:

- ☐ *Llapingachos* - Potato and cheese patties
- ☐ *Seco de borrego* - Stewed lamb over rice
- ☐ *Seco de chivo* - Stewed goat over rice
- ☐ *Hornado* - Slow roasted pork
- ☐ *Fritada* - Fried pork
- ☐ *Cuy* - Guinea pig

Insider's Guide

- *Maitos* - Chicken, fish or grubs roasted in bijao leaves

Soups:

- *Locro de papas* - Thick potato soup
- *Bolón de verde* - Soup with plantain dumplings
- *Caldo de pata* - Cow hoof soup
- *Caldo de pollo* - Chicken soup often served with chicken feet
- *Ceviche* - Cold seafood soup
- *Fanesca* - Seasonal Easter soup

Seafood:

- *Camarones al ajillo* - Garlic shrimp
- *Encocados* - Seafood cooked in coconut milk

Side dishes:

- *Mote* - Hominy
- *Menestra* - Stewed beans or lentils

- ☐ *Patacones* - Double fried green plantains
- ☐ *Yuca* - Potato-like tuber
- ☐ *Ají* - Ecuadorian hot sauce

Snacks/Desserts:

- ☐ *Bizcochos* - Crunchy, buttery bread sticks
- ☐ *Helados de paila* - Fruit juice ice cream made is special copper bowls
- ☐ *Melcocha* - Sugar cane taffy
- ☐ *Dulce de higos* - Figs cooked with panela served with cheese
- ☐ *Maduros con queso* - Sweet plantains with cheese and mayo
- ☐ *Chochos* - white beans served with toasted maize and onions
- ☐ *Pan de yuca* - Cheese and yuca breads often served with yogurt
- ☐ *Humitas* - Corn puree similar to tamales
- ☐ *Quimbolitos* - Sweet cakes with raisins cooked in leaves

Insider's Guide

- *Empanadas* - Bread filled with cheese topped with sugar
- *Empanadas de verde* - Plantain dough filled with cheese, chicken, etc.
- Chocolate made in Ecuador - try Kallari, Pacari or Republica de Cacao

Drinks:

- *Morocho* - Thick corn drink flavored with cinnamon and raisins
- *Chicha* - Fermented drink made from chonta, yuca or corn
- *Jugo de caña* - Fresh sugarcane juice
- *Guayusa* tea
- *Caipiriñas* - Limeade with sugar cane liqueur
- *Canelazo* - Hot cinnamon tea with naranjilla and aguardiente
- *Colada morada* - Seasonal purple fruit drink made for Day of the Dead

Section Four

On the Road

While traveling in Ecuador follow these tips to get the most out of your trip and avoid problems.

"NOT ALL THOSE WHO WANDER ARE LOST"

– J.R.R. TOLKIEN

Chapter Thirteen

What to Keep with You

Now that the planning's done, let's get going!

While loading up the car or bus, make sure you have the following things with you at all times.

Documents

Make sure that you have several copies of your passport with you at all times. It's a good idea to keep them in a couple of different places (i.e. don't put them all in one piece of luggage) so that if something happens you have a copy.

You are required as a tourist to show your passport with valid visa anytime you are asked by the police (if you get stopped at a police check in your car, they will almost certainly ask for it). Also, if you lose your passport or if it is stolen, a copy will help expedite the replacement process at the embassy.

Toilet Paper and Soap

Bathrooms on the road aren't always fully stocked, so it's good to have what you need with you.

At some public restrooms, there will be a person outside charging for use of the bathrooms. It usually costs about 15 cents and includes toilet paper, but there isn't always soap. It's good to have some loose change on hand.

Liquid hand sanitizer can be really handy too. If you need to buy some in Ecuador, ask at the pharmacies.

Maps

I like to have several maps with me to compare them. It's also a good idea to get hold of city maps of any big cities you will be going through, especially Quito, Guayaquil and Cuenca.

For maps of smaller cities and towns the Lonely Planet guidebook has great little maps of the main drag of most places.

Some rental car companies do offer GPS devices for

Insider's Guide

an additional cost. You can also download GPS apps on your phone that can be helpful.

"Maps.ME was a useful offline map app for our travels, especially while in the city. Google Maps also has the ability to download sections for offline use."
- *Jen Mitchell*

Snacks and Water

I've already mentioned that vendors will be getting on and off the bus constantly, but that doesn't mean they will be selling what you want. Plus, not everything for sale on the bus is safe to eat.

If you're driving yourself, snacks and water are very important. We have found that sometimes there are long stretches of road where there is NO FOOD. Maybe you can find some little stores, but for that you have to find a town. Having snacks in the car can be a lifesaver, and you should always have bottled water with you.

Ecuador Road Trip

Entertainment

If you can read in the car/bus take a book with you.

We like to play an Ecuadorian version of the license plate game. In Ecuador, the first letter of the license plate represents the province where the plate was issued (it's usually the first letter of the province, like "Pichincha" plates start with a "P"). Try to find 23 different letters (there are 24 provinces, but I don't think you'll find a plate from the Galapagos).

Another game we play is spotting waterfalls--any size waterfall counts. You could play the same game with volcanoes. :)

Camera

You will see lots of spots where you'll want to snap photos. Keep your camera ready!

Here are a couple of tips:

- The sky will often come out white since on the Equator the sun spends so much time above your head. The professional tip of trying to keep the sun behind you just isn't

Insider's Guide

    always possible. Try to take more photos early in the day and later in the afternoon.

- Another reason to start picture taking early is that clouds often come in the afternoon, especially in the mountains. For a great view of those impressive volcanoes try to get photos in the morning hours. Early in the morning the mountains seem to sparkle.

- Watch for power lines when taking photos. I've had many a photo spoiled by power lines and I usually don't realize they are there until I see the print on the computer. :(

Ecuadorians are super friendly, but many are also very shy. If you ask to take their photo (or one of their child) they will usually say yes, but if you take their photo without asking they will probably get very self-conscious.

Chapter Fourteen

Hotel Tips

As part of your planning, it's a good idea to make hotel reservations as you travel. I mentioned before that you might not want to make concrete plans too far ahead due to a variety of things that could slow you down.

In most cases you can make reservations the night before. Exceptions to this rule are during holidays, especially at popular destinations.

If you are unsure about how far you will be able to travel the next day, don't sweat it. You can call a few hours ahead and save a room or just show up. Even if the hotel you had thought to stay in is full, they will be happy to refer you to a nearby option.

Motel vs Hotel

When choosing a place to stay it helps to understand how common lodging terms are translated in Ecuador.

Hostal: This term often brings up images of basic

Insider's Guide

rooms. Maybe even dirty rooms. However, hostals in Ecuador are small, budget hotels. Many are very nice and clean.

Hotel: These are larger buildings. Many lack personality. Hotels are available at all price points, from budget to luxury options. In the big cities, a hotel is usually more expensive.

Motel: You may be imagining a small, old-fashioned, dirty place when talking about a motel. In Ecuador, motels are "love nests". Many are available by the hour. Some even have garages, so that people can drive in and shut the door behind them with no one being able to see their car parked outside.

Hosteria: Hosterias tend to be pricier and have more amenities. They often are located on large pieces of land with lots of gardens around them.

Haciendas: Old colonial structures that have been converted into lodging for tourists. Most of the haciendas in Ecuador are relatively expensive.

The majority of lodging options include breakfast either in the price or for an additional cost. You will also find free WIFI with decent signal at most accommodations.

Showers

After a long day of traveling, you make it to your hotel. The first thing that you may want to do is to shower. Do you know how the shower works?

First, "H" stands for cold (*helado*) and "C" for hot (*caliente*).

More than likely the hot water is provided by a tankless, on-demand, gas water heater. To get hot water:

1. Turn the hot water on full blast.
2. Let the water run for a few minutes.
3. Check to see if water is hot--I wouldn't even get undressed until you are sure you've got some heat.
4. Once water is hot, add small amounts of cold water until the water is at your preferred temperature.

While you are showering, the water temp will probably vary. Slowly adjust the cold water only.

Insider's Guide

If the water gets steadily colder and all the cold water is off, you may need to hurry up and finish bathing. There is little hope of the water getting hot again once it starts going cold.

If you can't get the water hot in the beginning, talk to the front desk. We have been in hotels that don't turn the hot water on until guests sign in and it can take a while for the system to be ready to use.

Another issue can be that the gas tanks have run out and the hotel workers haven't realized it. This is usually a quick fix and someone will let you know when you can try the shower again.

Electric Showers

This shower option is less and less common at hotels in Ecuador, but you may run across it when staying with friends or at smaller accommodations outside of the city.

For electric showers, there is usually just one knob.

1. Make sure the breaker switch is on (Remember-- "up" doesn't necessary mean "on").

2. Turn on the water. Turn it on pretty hard until you hear the water heating shower head turn on. If water pressure is really low it won't kick on.

3. Once you feel the warm water, adjust your temperature. More water will mean a colder shower. Less water makes the water hotter.

When taking a hot shower do not touch the area on top of the shower head or the metal pipe connected to it--danger!

Toilet Paper

While we are on the subject of bathrooms, I'd just like to mention that it is customary in Ecuador to throw used toilet paper in the waste bin and not in the toilet. Often hotels will have instructions posted on how they want you to dispose of toilet paper. Follow their instructions.

Lodging Safety

It's a good idea not to leave valuables or documents (especially your passport) in your hotel room--most hotels will have a safe at the front desk.

Insider's Guide

Chapter Fifteen

Parking the Car

Before settling into your hotel room for the night, make sure your rental car is safe.

When checking into a hotel ask what parking options they have. In big cities, it's a good idea to make sure there are parking options before you even make your reservations.

Most hotels will have one of the following options:

- Their own lot
- A shared lot that they partner with
- Suggestions for a public lot

When leaving your car in a public lot, it's preferable to leave it in a guarded or fully enclosed lot, especially when parking overnight.

Public lots will charge by the hour or by the day.

In bigger cities, we have opted to leave the car in the lot the entire time we are in the city. It can be easier to travel by taxi or on foot than deal with the traffic and narrow, one-way streets.

When parking the car for the night, unload the car completely. Don't leave anything in sight that could tempt thieves.

Parking on the Street

While traveling or at hotels, your only parking option may be to park on the street.

Ask your hotel what the rules are for parking on the street.

In Cuenca, my dad got a parking ticket. The spots are free overnight, but he didn't realize that starting at 7 a.m. you have to pay.

Paid parking spaces don't usually have meters like you may be used to seeing. There is a parking attendant that you must track down and pay, then place the receipt they give you in the car window.

When parking on the street as you travel, try to park where you can see the car and don't leave things in clear view.

Chapter Sixteen

Precautions

I really want you to enjoy your trip, so here are a few things to keep in mind so that you stay safe and healthy.

Health Issues

Water: There are some areas in Ecuador that have clean tap water, but not everywhere. To be safe, drink bottled water.

For the most part restaurants buy ice made with clean water, but if they make their own ice they may be using tap water.

Food: As is true anywhere, you can get sick eating undercooked eggs or meat in Ecuador. If you like your meat on the rare side, it's advisable while you are visiting Ecuador to order everything "medium well." There are some very nice five-star restaurants in Quito and Guayaquil where the food is perfectly safe--and they will still only cook your steak to "medium well."

Ecuador Road Trip

Fresh fruit and vegetables should be washed before eating. While in Ecuador, you can buy KILOL or similar products to disinfect fruit or veggies that you will eat without peeling or cooking. It is not advisable to buy fruit that has already been cut up on the street, as you have no way of knowing how clean the utensils used to prepare it were.

Ecuador is famous for its wonderful variety of juices. They are available at every restaurant and along the streets in side stalls. Unless you are absolutely certain that the juice has been made with filtered water, don't order it. Juices made with unclean water will make you VERY sick, VERY quickly.

Sun: The sun on the equator is strong, even though the air is cool. I once was wearing tights on a cloudy day in the mountains and got sunburned on my legs.

Protect your skin and eyes from the sun.

Altitude: As you travel, you will go up and down in altitude. If you begin to feel lightheaded or get a headache, it's a good idea to lay down and rest. Drinking plenty of water will help your body adjust.

Ocean: Some beaches have occasional rip tides

Insider's Guide

(Atacames is especially known for them). Ask locals about areas to avoid. If you are caught in a riptide, swim parallel to the shore until you swim out of it. Many beaches do not have lifeguards, so if you are not a strong swimmer, stay close to the shore.

Dangers on the Road

The roads in Ecuador have improved A LOT! In place of dirt roads there are now multi-lane highways. You should still drive carefully though.

As you go up and down the mountains the roads curve around and around. There are hardly any super straight roads in the whole country.

Watch for:

- Unexpected potholes.
- Real and fake speed bumps. We were recently driving in the jungle down the main Highway 35. There were constant signs warning of speed bumps, so we would slow down, only to find that there was no speed bump. Just when we started to doubt the signs, a real speed bump appeared and sent

us flying.

- People and animals on the road. We've seen pigs, cows, horses, and dogs on the roads. Some appear out of nowhere. People also walk along the edge of the roads.

The weather can affect road conditions. Fog is common, especially at higher elevations. (Fun fact-- when you are driving through "fog" in the mountains, chances are that you are really driving through clouds!) Drive slowly. You will come across other drivers without their lights on. Some may even try to pass you no matter how dense the fog is.

If there is lots of rain, another danger can be landslides. Sometimes sections of road will close down because of landslides or threats of one.

I've already mentioned crazy drivers. Watch for motorcycles as well. In the cities, they like to weave in and out to get through traffic and they have no aversion to passing you on the right.

If you are the pedestrian, also, be careful. Many drivers view a stop sign as a suggestion and, even if they do stop, they cruise right through the crosswalk before stopping completely.

Insider's Guide

Cows on the road in Mindo

When walking also beware of uneven sidewalks and "land mines" left by dogs.

Meeting the Police

The police will set up checkpoints. Some are permanent checkpoints; others are random.

When talking to the police, be friendly. They are usually looking for drivers without licenses or for drugs, so they will probably just check your passport, license and the car's registration. Keep these documents with you whenever you drive. You never know when you will be asked to show them.

Ecuador Road Trip

In Quito, there is a special program called *"Pico y Placa"* (Peak and Plate). Each day of the work week, license plates ending in a certain number are not allowed to drive in downtown Quito during peak hours.

Affected vehicles cannot drive from 7 a.m. until 9:30 a.m. and from 4 p.m. until 7:30 p.m. The schedule is as follows:

- On **Monday** license plates ending in 1 or 2
- On **Tuesday** license plates ending in 3 or 4
- On **Wednesday** plates ending in 5 or 6
- On **Thursday** plates ending in 7 or 8
- On **Friday** plates ending in 9 or 0

How big of a deal is this? The fine you pay if you violate *"pico y placa"* is very high and your car can be impounded until the peak hours are over.

Most rental car agencies will have you sign a document saying you understand this law. Don't drive your car thinking you can tempt fate (or talk yourself out of it if you get caught). *Pico y Placa* is the most enforced traffic law in Quito and they will bust

Insider's Guide

you!

Getting Lost

In Ecuador, many roads have little or no signage. This situation is improving, but you still may get off on a wrong road.

If you aren't sure where you are going or where to go next, ask someone for directions. With that information, ask someone else. My dad likes to "survey" people, because we have had several experiences following the first set of directions only to find out that the person didn't actually know the way to go.

So, ask two, three or more people and follow the directions that are similar.

Another way to avoid getting lost is avoiding some of the big cities, if possible. Many cities have bypass routes that take you around the city instead of through it. Having those city maps helps too.

Chapter Seventeen
Some *Friendly* Tips

As you travel remember a few things. First, this is a foreign country. They don't always do things the way we do. This doesn't make their way wrong, it's just different.

Ecuadorians are very friendly and welcoming of people from other countries. I hope it always stays that way!

Patience

One of the things that can be hard to understand is the "*mañana*" mentality. Just about anything can wait until later and most things will take longer than you expect. Since we are used to fast paced life this can be annoying.

Patience is a good thing. Plus, you're on vacation. Just roll with it.

Insider's Guide

Greetings

An essential part of the Ecuadorian culture is the initial greeting. Whether you enter a store, board a bus or just pass someone on the street, you should say hello and smile.

When being introduced to someone it is customary to shake hands. Young ones and friends will greet women with a kiss (a "*besito*") on the cheek.

English

Remember that the official language of Ecuador is Spanish. If someone doesn't understand what you say in English, raising your voice will not help.

If you struggle with Spanish, don't worry. As I've said before, Ecuadorians are friendly and patient. They appreciate your efforts to speak their language.

That said, there are many people in Ecuador that **do** speak English, especially those attending universities and those working in the tourism industry. It may seem easy to complain in English among ourselves, but someone may hear and understand you. Don't say anything you wouldn't want understood.

Ecuadorians watch lots of English movies with subtitles, so most people know and recognize common swear words.

Tipping

There can be a lot of confusion when it comes to tipping. Although tipping is not near as common as it is in other parts of the world, it is nice to leave a tip.

Some restaurants will add the tip to your bill. It will be noted as "*Servicio*". Others don't. If you want to leave a tip, it is typical to leave 8-10%.

Drivers of metered taxis may charge you more than what is on the meter. This is usually because your ride didn't reach the base price, which is usually around $1.50 depending on the city. It is also customary to round the odd cents up to the nearest 5 or 10 cents.

Insider's Guide

Bartering

Bartering at markets is expected, but don't go overboard. Remember that merchants are working hard and providing for their families with the proceeds from their products.

A good way to know if you are getting a good price is to ask several vendors the price of the same item. Also, if you walk away and they lower the price you know you haven't gone too cheap.

In shops with price tags, it isn't common to barter.

Disparaging Remarks

Ecuadorians like to talk politics and you can easily be drawn into negative talk. Just remember that you won't make friends by talking badly about their government or by always pointing out that "our" way is better.

All in all, let's try to endear ourselves to the people by being patient and respectful. They in turn will continue to welcome us into their beautiful country.

Chapter Eighteen
Have a Great Time!

Do you have "travel-fever"? I sincerely hope you come to explore this beautiful country, that you have an amazing vacation and that you come to love Ecuador as much as I do. And....

I would love to hear about your adventure!

On my website: Life-in-Ecuador.com, I write about my adventures and I would love to add yours too! You can contact me there or submit your story directly on the "Share with Us > Your Ecuador Stories" page.

Save while Traveling Ecuador

A few years ago, I started a discount travel program here in Ecuador called Ecuador VIP. If your trip includes any of the places that currently have VIP Partners, feel free to contact me. Mention the promo code: "Road Trip Book" and I'll give you one for FREE!

Insider's Guide

Special Thanks

The following people helped me immensely to prepare this book and I want to say "Thank You" to each and every one!

Editor

Cynthia Maloy

Cover and Map Designs

Tasha Riedman

Launch Team

Valentine Riedman IV	Val Riedman III
Chelsea Price	Vlad Litvinov
Regina Potenza	Mark Brooker
Joellen Nienaber	Jen Mitchell
Margit Streifeneder	Josh Lewis
Jo Farmer	Andrew Sudron
Todd Gorishek	Beth Riedman
Nicole Frank	Tracey Mussett
Charline Ahlgreen	Sharon Riedman
Tobias Alexander	Carrie Lewis
Elyette Maillet	Kelly Harding
Heidi Duran	

Ecuador Road Trip

Thank YOU for Reading My Book!

I really appreciate all feedback and would love to hear what you thought!

Please, please, please leave a helpful review on Amazon letting me know your opinion of what you've read!

Thanks a million!
Jessamyn Salinas

Made in the USA
Middletown, DE
18 December 2017